LIFE IN COLONIAL AMERICA

THE CITY IN COLONIAL AMERICA

L. H. COLLIGAN

Cavendish
Square
New York

Published in 2015 by Cavendish Square Publishing, LLC
243 5th Avenue, Suite 136, New York, NY 10016

CPSIA Compliance Information: Batch # WS14CSQ

All websites were available and accurate when this book was sent to press.

Library of Congress Cataloging-in-Publication Data
Colligan, L. H.
The city in colonial america / L.H. Colligan.
pages cm. — (Life in colonial America)
Includes bibliographical references and index.
ISBN 978-1-62712-882-7 (hardcover) ISBN 978-1-62712-884-1 (ebook)
1. Colonial cities—North America—Juvenile literature. 2. Cities and towns—United States—History—Juvenile literature. 3. City and town life—United States—History—Juvenile literature. 4. United States—Social life and customs—To 1775—Juvenile literature. 5. United States—History—Colonial period, ca. 1600-1775—Juvenile literature. I. Title.

HT123.C584 2014
307.760973—dc23

2013050649

Editorial Director: Dean Miller
Editor: Fletcher Doyle
Senior Copy Editor: Wendy A. Reynolds
Art Director: Jeffrey Talbot
Designer: Joseph Macri
Production Editor: David McNamara
Production Manager: Jennifer Ryder-Talbot
Photo Research: J8 Media

Printed in the United States of America

Contents

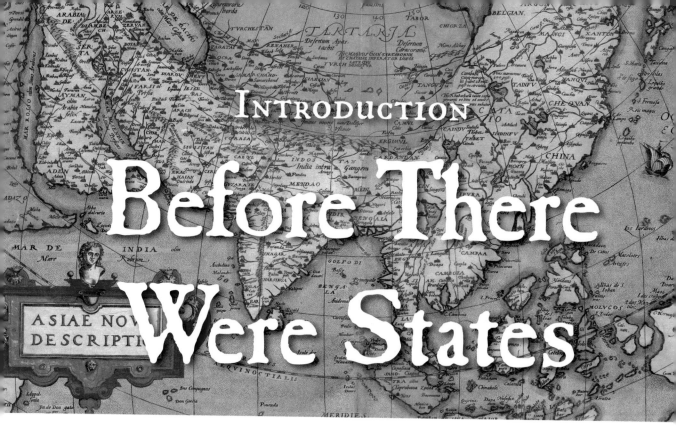

INTRODUCTION
Before There Were States

W hen Dutch explorer David de Vries said in 1642, "It is a pleasant and charming country, if only it were well peopled by our nation," he did not have to wait long for his wish to come true. The "pleasant and charming country" he found in the **New World** became "well peopled" just eleven years later. In 1653, New Amsterdam became a Dutch city in the New Netherlands colony. Eventually, New Amsterdam grew into New York City, one of the world's most important cities.

The Netherlands was not the only **Old World** nation to plant **colonies** in the New World. England, France, Norway, Portugal, Russia, Scotland, Spain, and Sweden did the same. By the late 1600s, cities anchored most of their colonies. These cities would become political centers where ideas about forming a united country took shape. These ideas led to the American Revolution and the founding of the United States in 1776.

This is the story of how America's cities came to be.

After Christopher Columbus spread the news of his 1492 transatlantic voyage, major European countries took notice. They went on shipbuilding binges and sent their own explorers across the Atlantic. They wanted to see for themselves the lands Columbus had described it this way to his Spanish **sponsors** in 1493:

> "Española is a marvel; the sierras and the mountains and the plains and the fields and the land are so beautiful and rich for planting and sowing, for raising all kinds of cattle, for building towns and villages. The harbours are beyond the belief of anyone who has not seen them, and the many great rivers give good waters of which the majority bear gold."

By the early 1500s, explorers such as Amerigo Vespucci, Giovanni da Verrazzano, and John Cabot travelled well beyond the lands Columbus had visited. In the **Western Hemisphere** they found vast oceans and great **continents** with millions of Native Americans living on them.

Waves of European and English explorers dropped anchor along the Atlantic and Caribbean coastlines throughout the 1500s. Some expeditions left the eastern coasts on horseback and headed into the interior. Along the way, European and English arrivals claimed forests, rivers, prairies, jungles, mountains, deserts, and shorelines for their home countries.

Others claimed, for their own religions, the Native Americans they met. A Spanish priest found a land teeming with new people to convert to Catholicism:

> "And all the land so far discovered is a beehive of people; it is as though God had crowded into these lands the great majority of mankind."
>
> —Bartolomé de Las Casas, 1542

This "beehive of people" had lived for thousands of years in settlements along the continents' waterways, forests, mountains, and deserts. They had cleared woodlands for farming. They had cut trails through woods and deserts for hunting and for trading with one another. They had built ceremonial buildings on sacred grounds and **pueblo** settlements on western lands. Yet Native Americans were strangers to European explorers, and European explorers were strangers to them.

Contact between these strangers proved fatal to Native Americans.

A significant percentage of the Native American population (estimates by historians of the native population in 1492 vary greatly) died early in the colonial period from European diseases they had never encountered before, and from which they had no protective immunity. After the massive reduction of their populations Native Americans left much behind: settlements, cleared lands, and a network of trading trails. As a result, **the Americas** were ripe for resettlement.

In 1620, English Pilgrims, the religious group that organized the Plymouth Colony, were among the first settlers to arrive. They constructed

New Amsterdam became New York when English soldiers conquered the city in 1664.

their settlement directly on the recently emptied Native American village called "Pawtuxet." The location offered access to good fishing waters, established farmlands, hunting grounds, and an excellent defensive position against enemies.

Other settlers from the Old World quickly followed. They founded small colonies, which the colonists governed as outposts of their home countries. Within one hundred years of 1492, the major European countries and England had all planted successful colonies in the Americas. From these colonies, major cities would arise, some within a colonist's single lifetime.

The Lost City

Basket by basket, workers in the Lost City carried soil great distances. They slowly built up more than one hundred earthen hills over many decades. The largest was about ten stories tall. On top, laborers constructed the city's most important building. It was likely a religious temple or the chief's residence. At the foot of the mound lay a fifty-acre public square. There, the city's inhabitants socialized, relaxed, heard public announcements, took part in ceremonies, and played games.

Anyone approaching the city by land or by river could spot the tallest mound from a distance. Strangers must have approached the city frequently because of its location. It was positioned at a spot where three rivers met—the Mississippi, Illinois, and the Missouri, as they would be called hundreds of years later.

The forgotten city had once been well known. In its golden age, from 700 BCE to 1400 CE, twenty thousand to forty thousand residents lived and worked in the **metropolis**. Its population included traders, government workers, builders, laborers, and farmers. People from settlements hundreds of miles away knew of the city's outstanding metal and stone hand tools for farming, copper jewelry, headdresses, and armor.

The city's traders controlled a wide network. They journeyed up and down the Mississippi River, trading with Great Lakes settlements to the north, and to the south, seaside settlements on the Gulf of Mexico. Their network of trails stretched as far as the eastern forests and western prairies.

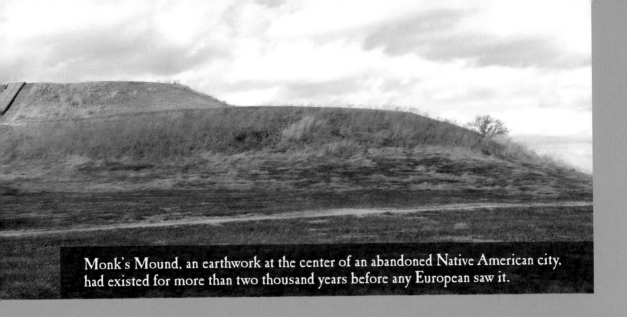

Monk's Mound, an earthwork at the center of an abandoned Native American city, had existed for more than two thousand years before any European saw it.

The timber circle marked astronomical events.

The city grew wealthy from manufacturing and trade. Its residents lived in separate upper- and middle-class neighborhoods. Wooden **palisade** fences and **bastion** watchtowers protected the city from possible attacks. Just outside the palisades, farmers grew crops to feed the hungry population.

Because of its organized government, the city's population grew as large as London's at the time. The **urban** settlement had all the features important American colonial cities would later possess. No one knows what disasters befell the Lost City. By 1400, it had become desolate. Perhaps disease, enemy attacks, overpopulation, overuse of farmland, and deforestation caused its collapse. Later, unrelated Native Americans who called themselves "Cahokians" settled in the area, but the once-grand city had long disappeared.

Later explorers who passed through knew nothing of the ancient city. Weather and time had worn down its mounds. The ancient buildings had sunk within them. Fortunately the remains of this lost city have been found and partially unearthed and restored. Tourists can now visit Cahokia, a United States Historical Monument located directly across the Mississippi from St. Louis, Missouri.

CHAPTER ONE

From Settlements to Cities

Native Americans welcomed Christopher Columbus with gifts when he set foot in the New World for the first time.

"The site and position of the towns should be selected in places where water is nearby and where it would be possible to demolish neighboring towns and properties in order to take advantage of the materials that are essential for building."
—Phillip II's The Laws of the Indies, No. 39

Christopher Columbus was known as an opinionated sailor, explorer, and adventurer. He also had firm opinions about how to settle a foreign colony. Settlers who founded colonies in what would become North, Central, and South America would follow similar plans to colonize the Americas. These basic ideas set the stage for colonial cities.

The first mainland colonial settlements were situated in "the most convenient places." In a land with trails but no real roads, the most convenient places to plant colonies were along waterfronts or existing Native American trails. These trails served as highways to move people, goods, and communications until actual roads could be built.

In southwest North America, Spaniards also found "the most convenient places" to locate their settlements. They established Albuquerque and Santa Fe near *El Camino Real* (The Royal Road). This ancient trail, spanning thousand of miles, connected Native American communities from *Tenochtitlán* (Mexico City) to the pueblos of northern New Mexico. It soon connected Spanish colonial cities.

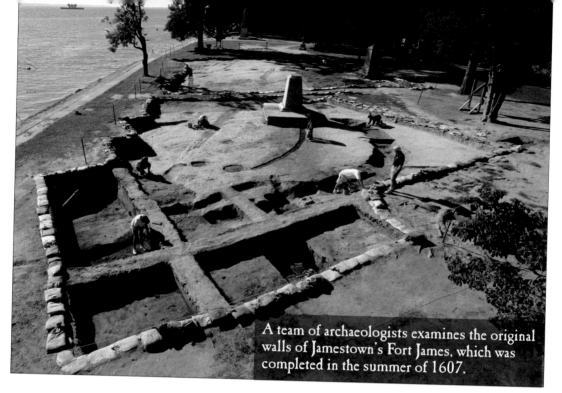

A team of archaeologists examines the original walls of Jamestown's Fort James, which was completed in the summer of 1607.

Columbus's "recipe" for colonial settlements stated that colonists must stick together for protection. Further, they needed to commit to a settlement by building their own houses within the colony's borders. Organized communities where many people live and work closely together in non-agricultural occupations become cities.

While Columbus never settled in the New World, he believed colonies required governments such as those in Europe. When people began to populate settlements in great numbers, they soon learned the importance of safety, roadways, clean water, and laws to deal with crowded conditions. As Columbus realized, people in settlements would need a government to make all this happen.

Columbus also recognized the importance of religion to colonists far from home. Traditional religious practices would help settlers to maintain the **culture** of

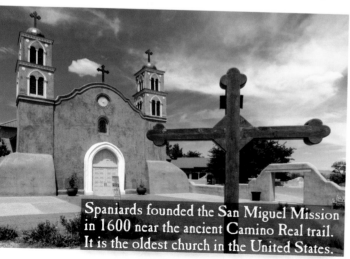

Spaniards founded the San Miguel Mission in 1600 near the ancient Camino Real trail. It is the oldest church in the United States.

their former homelands. Not long after Columbus wrote about the importance of churches as ceremonial gathering places, colonists of all nationalities and faiths built them in every colony. Churches, and **meetinghouses** also used as churches, were among the earliest and most important buildings at the center of colonial life.

A Tale of Three Cities

Mostly rural areas were populated in the New World of the 1600s. Even by the early 1700s only about five percent of the population lived in cities. However, a colony without a city was like a body without a heart. Colonial cities became centers for **commerce**. The function of these new cities was business, not farming.

Farmers and **plantation** owners came to the cities to sell or export their

Christopher Columbus's letter to the King and Queen of Spain, 1494

In obedience to your Highnesses' commands, and with submission to superior judgment, I will say whatever occurs to me in reference to the colonization and commerce of the Island of Española . . .

1. That in the said island there shall be founded three or four towns, situated in the most convenient places, and that the settlers who are there be assigned to the aforesaid places and towns.

2. That for the better and more speedy colonization of the said island, no one shall have liberty to collect gold in it except those who have taken out colonists' papers, and have built houses for their abode, in the town in which they are, that they may live united and in greater safety.

3. That each town shall have its alcalde [Mayor] ... and its **notary public**, as is the use and custom in Castile.

4. That there shall be a church, and parish priests or friars to administer the sacraments, to perform divine worship, and for the conversion of the Indians.

crops and livestock, and to buy goods they could not produce themselves. **Artisans** flocked to colonial cities to create tools, barrels, furniture, shoes, and other merchandise needed by those who lived in the country. City merchants ran shops to sell imported goods or goods manufactured nearby. Traders, along with those connected to shipping—shipbuilders, sailors, export agents, and others—crowded into urban centers. Lawyers, bookkeepers, and agents handled business documents. In the early 1700s, many inhabitants of all the American colonies owned African slaves. Most worked on farms, but ten to twenty percent worked in cities. Laborers of many nationalities immigrated to cities to load and unload ships and warehouses, construct buildings and streets, haul wood, clean houses, chimneys, and streets, or work as servants for prosperous city dwellers. Farmers and their families travelled from the countryside to worship at city churches. Above all, a city's public gathering places—its meetinghouses, churches, taverns, coffeehouses, and inns—brought people

In a single lifetime, some of the original settlers who had first lived in dugouts, huts, caves, and tents, spent their later lives in grand city houses.

Quaker William Penn, Philadelphia's founder, promoted peaceful acceptance of non-Quakers, including the local Lenape Native Americans.

together to exchange ideas, news, and gossip.

It is no surprise that the Bishop of London, in 1662, complained that Virginia Colony's failure to thrive was due to its lack of urban centers. He warned the colony's leaders: "It is easy to conclude that the only way of remedy for Virginia's disease . . . must be by procuring towns to be built . . ."

The next section will explore three thriving cities in America's colonies from their beginnings to the eve of the Declaration of Independence in 1776.

PHILADELPHIA

By 1770, Philadelphia was the largest colonial city in North America. Pehr (Peter) Kalm, a Swedish plant scientist, came to colonial America to collect seeds and plant specimens to bring back to Sweden. He not only collected plants, but a new friend: famed Philadelphian Benjamin Franklin. Following is Kalm's admiring account of Philadelphia as he remembered it in 1770.

From Settlements to Cities

A Visitor Remembers Philadelphia

"All the streets except two, which are nearest to the river, run in a straight line, and make right angles at the intersections. Some are paved, others are not; and it seems less necessary, since the ground is sandy, and therefore soon absorbs the wet. But in most of the streets is a pavement of flags, a fathom or more broad, laid before the houses, and posts put on the outside three or four fathom asunder. Under the roofs are gutters, which are carefully connected with pipes, and by this means, those who walk under them, when it rains, or when the snow melts, need not fear being wet by the dropping from the roofs.

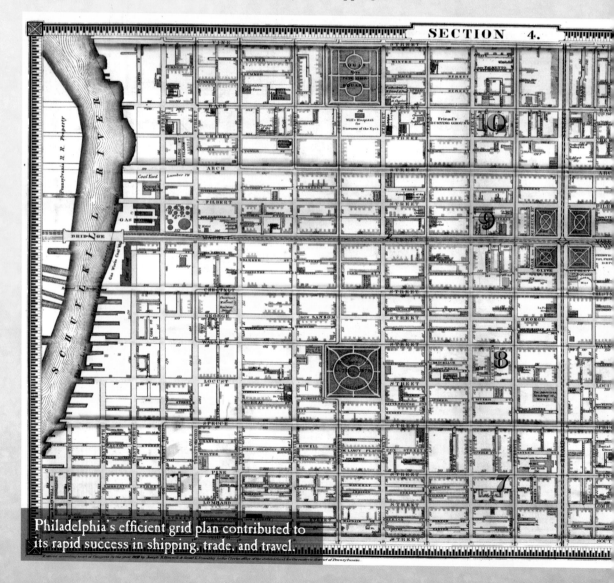

Philadelphia's efficient grid plan contributed to its rapid success in shipping, trade, and travel.

The houses make a good appearance, are frequently several stories high, and built either of bricks or of stone; but the former are more commonly used, since bricks are made before the town, and are well burnt. . . .This stone is now got in great quantities in the country, is easily cut, and has the good quality of not attracting the moisture in a wet season. . . . The town is now quite filled with inhabitants, which in regard to their country, religion, and trade, are very different from each other. You meet with excellent masters in all trades, and many things are made here full as well as in England. . . . Here is great plenty of provisions,

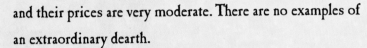

and their prices are very moderate. There are no examples of an extraordinary dearth.

Everyone who acknowledges God to be the Creator, preserver, and ruler of all things, and teaches or undertakes nothing against the state, or against the common peace, is at liberty to settle, stay, and carry on his trade here, be his religious principles ever so strange. No one is here molested on account of the erroneous principles of the doctrine, which he follows, if he does not exceed the above-mentioned bounds. And he is so well secured by the laws in his person and property, and enjoys such liberties, that a citizen of Philadelphia may in a manner be said to live in his house like a king.

On a careful consideration of what I have already said, it will be easy to conceive how this city should rise so suddenly from nothing, into such grandeur and perfection, without supposing any powerful monarch's contributing to it, either by punishing the wicked, or by giving great supplies in money. And yet its fine appearance, good regulations, agreeable situation, natural advantages, trade, riches and power, are by no means inferior to those of any, even of the most ancient towns in Europe."

—PETER KALM, 1770

An Exact Prospect of CHARLES TOWN.

CHARLES TOWN

Sailing **sloops** that carried crops from the rich farmlands surrounding
Philadelphia often travelled down the Atlantic coast to the major southern
seaport city in Charles Town (Charleston) in the Carolina Colony. Charles
Town planters devoted most of their wet lowlands to growing rice and indigo,
a then in-demand plant for the production of blue dye. As a result, the Carolina Colony imported food crops from other colonies.

During the 1700s, Charles Town served as a major trading colony with the West Indian colonies in the Caribbean. With many riches passing through, Charles Town harbor quickly became a magnet for pirates. In 1718, the famous pirate Blackbeard

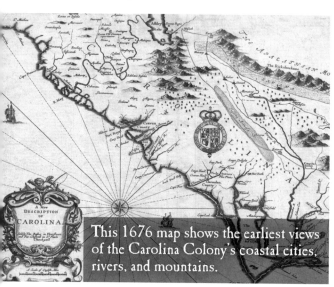
This 1676 map shows the earliest views of the Carolina Colony's coastal cities, rivers, and mountains.

Charles Town's riches lay within its fortified walls and the ships that sailed through its harbor in the 1760s.

blocked the harbor and stripped every entering and departing ship of cargo and passengers' belongings.

The 62-acre Charles Town, in 1730, was a walled city. The Spaniards, French, and Native Americans displaced from the area posed a threat to Charles Town. It had a desirable harbor and vast lands beyond its borders.

In the wet, marshy lowlands that made up the Carolina Colony, protective earth and brick walls encircled Charles Town. While other colonies used wooden palisade fencing, Charles Town's defenses likened to Europe's fortified towns. Fort-like bastions rose at each corner of the walls. A drawbridge spanned a moat.

By the mid-1700s Charles Town had outgrown its footprint and was ready to burst beyond its walls. The city needed more docks, warehouses, and stores. Charles Town's wealthy planters and merchants needed more room to build grand mansions and housing for servants and slaves. The protective walls had to come down, and they did so in 1730.

ALBUQUERQUE

The Spanish colonial cities of Albuquerque and Santa Fe, New Mexico, as well as Mexico City and Los Angeles, were constructed away from the ocean and huge rivers. All four cities boasted central plazas and **grid-pattern** streets. Spanish colonists located many of their cities in the midst of ancient Native American settlements. The reasons behind these possibly troubling decisions can be found in *The Laws of the Indies*. Spanish King Philip II published this city planner in 1573. The manual listed hundreds of rules which conquering Spanish explorers were ordered to follow when building settlements in the New World. It advised colonists to arrange paths in a grid pattern from a plaza anchored by an awe-inspiring church. The manual recommended the use of the same building materials and styles throughout each town. It directed colonists to set up farms and land for use by herding animals directly outside of cities. Albuquerque, New Mexico, was organized according to many of King Philip's plans as follows:

Do not select sites for towns in maritime locations
because of the danger that exists of pirates.

The main plaza is to be the starting point for the town. . .

The plaza should be square or rectangular . . . inasmuch as this shape is best for
fiestas in which horses are used and for any other fiestas that should be held.

In the plaza, no lots shall be assigned to private individuals; instead, they shall
be used for the buildings of the church and royal houses and for city use . . .

"The site and position of the towns should be selected in places
where water is nearby and where it would be possible to demolish
neighboring towns and properties in order to take advantage of
the materials that are essential for building."

They shall try as far as possible to have the buildings all of one type for the sake
of the beauty of the town.

The Laws of the Indies was successful as planned from the Spaniards' point of view. Unfortunately for the Native Americans, their well-organized pueblos were no match for the size and power of Spanish colonial cities, which dominated the pueblos. Cities that followed the *Laws of the Indies* remain in North America today. Central plazas, awe-inspiring churches, government buildings, and consistent Spanish architecture survive in the old centers of Albuquerque and Santa Fe, New Mexico.

Santa Fe's Palace of the Governors, built in 1618, is the oldest continuously used government building in the United States.

CHAPTER TWO

Public and Private Spaces

Since the 1630s, the Boston Common has served as a cow pasture, a burial ground, a military camp, and a public park.

"Within the town, a commons shall be delimited, large enough that although the population may experience a rapid expansion, there will always be sufficient space where the people may go to for recreation and take their cattle to pasture without them making any damage."
—PHILLIP II's THE LAWS OF THE INDIES, NO. 39

When settlers founded the first colonies, townspeople lived close together for convenience and for protection from Native American attacks. Settlement leaders assigned inhabitants closely spaced lots along a main path with a grassy area in the center. This layout resembled village plans in England, Spain, and Holland.

Houses were constructed to stand closely together, usually to the edge of the main path. Families of the time were large, and the first colonial houses were small. Meeting places outside of the home needed to be designed and built. There was little to no land space for cows, sheep, and goats to graze. The townspeople needed a building in which they could worship together or conduct private and town business. From the beginning, colonists created public spaces to meet those needs.

THE COMMONS: A VERY OLD IDEA

The Old World custom of setting aside public green space goes back to the Middle Ages (1066–1485). During that time such open spaces could be found

As villages grew, the town commons, like this one in 1830 Concord, Massachusetts, continued as the center of village life.

on royal estates. In exchange for the crops and livestock they raised for a royal lord, peasants had an important right. The lord of the estate had to grant permission for them to use grazing land. This land was called "The **Commons**."

When Old World settlers established colonies in the Americas, many continued the custom of The Commons. The Commons provided colonial town families a way to keep a few animals without owning a farm. It also served as a central place where neighbors could easily meet in public. The Commons, as well as town squares and plazas, gave colonial settlements unity and identity.

Town commons are still valuable public assets in the towns and cities that maintained them. Many colonial-era town commons have been preserved, not for the grazing of animals but for the recreation of a city's residents.

THE CITY IN COLONIAL AMERICA

The Meetinghouse

From a distance, a newcomer approaching any American colonial city in the 1600s and early 1700s would first see its tallest or largest building. In a non-English colonial city such as Albuquerque, that building would have been a church. In the English **Puritan** colonies of New England, the tallest building would be the meetinghouse. Colonists managed the city's business there during the week. On Sundays and holy days the building was used as a place of worship.

Colonists built their meetinghouses as soon as they completed the construction of their defenses and private homes. The townspeople usually located their meetinghouses on the town commons or at a crossroads. As one New

Englander boasted, his town's meetinghouse was: " . . . framed by our own hammers and saws, and by our own hands set in the convenientest place for us all."

Meetinghouses served several purposes. Before the creation of formal governments, colony leaders used the meetinghouse to discuss town business. Announcements townspeople needed to read were posted on the meetinghouse doors. As towns started to grow into cities, businesspeople gathered at the meetinghouse.

In contrast to the traditional awe-inspiring Spanish churches—which held bell towers, arches, stained glass, and statues—meetinghouses were plain. Most were built in a square shape and topped with a pyramid roof. Their windows were first made of oiled paper, then later, clear glass. The wooden meetinghouses were unheated because fire was always viewed as a danger during colonial times.

Before Sunday services, worshipers entered through one of three doors. The minister's family and important visitors came through the front door. Females entered through one side door, males through the other. The elderly, as well as wealthy families, though not their restless boys, sat in box

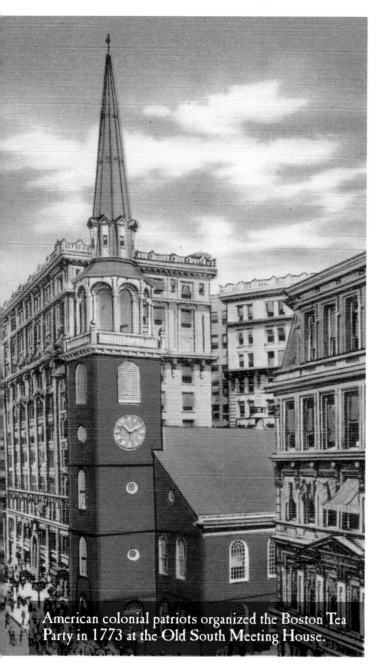

American colonial patriots organized the Boston Tea Party in 1773 at the Old South Meeting House.

pews that were set up in the downstairs level. Slaves, servants, single males, boys, and females sat on separate sides in the upstairs "gallery" pews.

Worship services lasted most of Sunday. Ministers delivered sermons that lasted many hours, so worshipers needed a long noon intermission. During the break, they might have found warmth, food, and conversation at a nearby Sabbath "Sabbady" or "noon house." These nearby low buildings served as horse stables. Quiet conversation was allowed, though children could not play or talk too casually. Everyone returned to church for the afternoon service to sing hymns and listen to more long sermons. Church officials stood by the doors to make sure no one headed home early.

Early Swedish settlers in the Pennsylvania Colony modeled their first homes on the log cabins of their home country.

The Warmth of Home

New World colonists who first lived in caves, huts, and tents must have longed to build the kinds of houses and villages they remembered from their homelands. Many of the first real houses built resembled those they had become accustomed to in the Old World.

Soon, though, townspeople of different nationalities began to feel the stirrings of their New World identity. They added unique features to their houses, which made them more than copies of the structures back home. Many American colonial houses added lean-to spaces—buildings that are attached on the side of larger buildings—as families and fortunes expanded.

Thatched roofs made of grasses like those in England gave way to wooden shingled roofs in American colonies. Cellars in English houses were uncommon but not in those of New England. In a cold climate, cellars were useful for winter food storage. This changed diets since colonists could eat from their cool stores of nutritious vegetables, meats, milk, and cheeses throughout the winter. This belowground storage gave way to longer selling seasons for farmers. Cellars insulated houses better than those set into the ground like those back in England. This meant colonists used less firewood. Family budgets could be used for other purposes.

Prosperous New England families of the 1700s could afford houses with features like those in the Paul Revere House in Boston—an addition, a slate roof, and casement windows.

To keep pace with the housing needs of immigrants arriving in droves from Europe and England, master carpenters from the Old World were both welcomed and prized. They came with their tools common to England and found plenty of work. Immigrant English carpenters readily adapted to local materials and needs of the colonists. Towns developing into cities required sturdy houses that could be quickly built and placed close together. Housing plans became simplified; lean-to additions could be attached to the rear of homes at a later time.

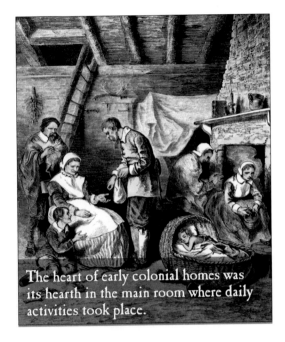

The heart of early colonial homes was its hearth in the main room where daily activities took place.

In early colonial homes, most rooms did not have a specific purpose. One day a space might be a parlor, the next it might be used as a sleeping area for a visiting relative. Most historical houses seen today give visitors the impression that colonial houses were filled with porcelain dishes, silver candlesticks, and mahogany dressers and beds. Only the wealthy colonists, from the late seventeenth and into the eighteenth centuries, filled their grand homes with elegant furnishings.

Most colonists slept on bedrolls, which they put away during the day. A dining table was likely to be a few rough boards with a bench or stools stored beneath. The term "room and board" refers to colonial table boards. If the household owned a chair—which many did not—only the head of the house sat in it. The expression "chairman of the board" came from colonial times.

Most houses had a ground-floor main room called the "hall," similar to houses in England. Since people needed to be near a source of heat and light, everyone gathered by the main fireplace in the hall. Privacy was in short supply since most family activities happened there. Colonial halls were the first living rooms. There, colonists prayed, cooked, ate, read, worked on mending, knitting, quilting, and kept warm.

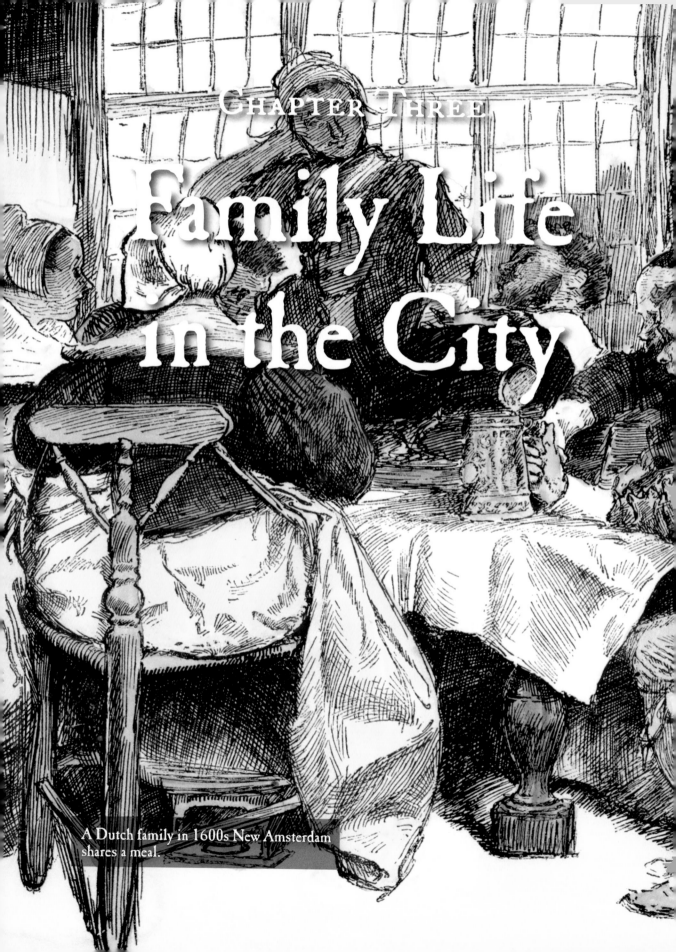

CHAPTER THREE
Family Life in the City

A Dutch family in 1600s New Amsterdam shares a meal.

"Families are the nurseries of society and
the first combination of Mankind"
—COTTON MATHER, 1658

Northern colonists who settled near the Atlantic coast were mainly in their thirties and forties and came over as family groups. They shared the same nationality, English or Dutch language, and religion. For them, families represented the colony's future. The New England colonists viewed the family as the primary unit of social control. Thus, they expected every individual to be a part of a household. In fact, Connecticut passed a law stating that single men could not live alone without the settlement's permission. They were pressured to board with families and marry soon. Divorce existed, but it was rare regardless of a husband's or wife's misbehavior.

The high value the Northern and Middle Atlantic Colonies of New York, New Jersey, Delaware, and Pennsylvania placed on families led to high birthrates. A family could typically have from eight to a dozen children. To make room for new babies, it was the custom of many colonial city parents to send their teenage children off to live with other families—perhaps in the countryside—or with relatives who had a trade to teach them.

From 1630 to 1700 the population of the Massachusetts Bay Colony alone increased from 10,000 to 100,000 people. Equally dramatic growth was true for the family-oriented, **immigration**-friendly Dutch and the English **Quakers** in the Pennsylvania Colony. By 1700, America had five major colonial cities: Boston, Newport, New Amsterdam, Philadelphia, and Charles Town—the only sizeable southern city with a large population during the colonial period.

Southern Colonial Families

Southern population growth was sluggish for much of the colonial period. A small number of wealthy plantation-owning families were similar in structure to those in the Northern Colonies, but they were few. These families mainly lived on plantations throughout the Virginia, Georgia, and Carolina colonies. Country families intermarried to keep property in the hands of related families. Plantations produced cash crops such as tobacco, rice, and indigo for export. Some planters kept grand townhouses in the cities where they conducted plantation-related business with traders, shippers, and merchants. But the economic engine that fueled the Southern Colonies was rural agriculture, not urban business.

Another drag on southern population growth related to immigration. More single male immigrants than families kept the Southern Colonies small, as they arrived as **indentured servants**. They worked under **contract** for wealthy planters who paid for their passage to North America. Indentured servants, over a period of five to seven years, worked off the debt of their ship passage. During that time they usually could not marry. Fewer female indentured servants came to the Southern Colonies so there was a shortage of women for southern men to marry.

The south colonies' climate bred an unhealthy environment, which also slowed population growth. Mosquito-borne diseases such as malaria and yellow fever were far deadlier in the tropical climate of the Maryland, Virginia, Georgia, and Carolina colonies than in the Mid-Atlantic and Northern Colonies. Southern families suffered more infant and childhood deaths than did those in the north. Without a growing population, Southern Colonies were unable to develop early cities except for Charles Town. They eventually turned to the slave system when immigration and families could not supply the labor force plantations needed.

SLAVES IN THE CITIES

Ten to twenty percent of colonial slaves worked in cities instead of on plantations. Their northern masters bought them from slave traders in the West Indies and the Southern Colonies. In the city, most slaves worked in households or as artisans in shops. Female slaves mainly labored as domestic servants or in laundries. They tended their owners' houses, cooked, and cared for their children. Urban slave owners put their male slaves to work as gardeners, coach drivers, house servants, sailors, and dockworkers. Some owners "rented out" their slaves to merchants and artisans and collected the slaves' pay for themselves. In the city, slaves were usually better clothed, fed, and educated than those in the country.

However, urban slaves had one great disadvantage when it came to forming families. To increase their labor force, Southern plantation owners urged slaves to have children, usually with slaves who lived on the same plantation. Urban slaves did not belong to slave communities where they might form relationships and have children. Instead, they were relegated to stifling attic rooms, stable lofts, or the back rooms of laundries and the stores where they worked. There they lived singly or perhaps with just one or two other slaves.

Urban slaves experienced better working conditions than rural slaves but missed out on the community life of the plantation.

Kemble

Fortunately, many urban slaves had learned to read. Some had worked alongside their masters in shops and businesses. When they gained their freedom, many former urban slaves found employment or started businesses. This advancement meant they could finally start their own families.

Spanish Colonial Families

The Spanish colonies, during the 1500s, at first suffered the same slow population growth as the southern Atlantic colonies, and for the same reason: the first Spanish settlers were overwhelmingly male. Few Spanish families were willing to travel into the distant, rugged wilderness of southwest North America. Those who did created a slave or indentured servant system using Native Americans to work on Spanish ranches in the New World. These few founding families became wealthy and soon controlled vast Native American territories. But the number of such ranching families was small. Spanish colonies needed more Spaniards. Their colonies needed cities for trading and manufacturing.

Spanish men found a solution to their population problem. They began to have children with the Native American women whose peoples they had conquered. Back in Spain, the king and church leaders disapproved, ordering settlers to bring families from Spain to the New World. They told the men to return to Spain every two years, but the orders were ignored. Because the colonists were too far away to be controlled, the unmarried familial relationships with Native American females continued.

Government and church leaders back in Spain finally gave in, ceasing to control the relationships. They needed their colonial populations to grow, work the land, and organize cities for trade. They wanted Native people to become **Catholics** and owe their loyalty to Spain. They wanted colonists to plant Spanish traditions in the New World. This could only be done through families. Royal and church leaders reluctantly allowed male Spanish settlers to intermarry with the Native American women. The result led to a booming population. The Spanish colonial cities of Albuquerque and Santa Fe soon followed.

A few Spanish families owned vast ranches long after Spain gave up its New World colonies.

The powerful Spanish Catholic Church thought of families as small kingdoms below the more important kingdoms of God and church. **Patriarchal** family authority began with God, flowed down through church authorities, to a father, then down to his wife, children, and household servants. Spanish parents did not always welcome religious influence over family decisions. They frequently arranged marriages for their children in order to strengthen relationships with other families. When parents tried to force a marriage, priests sometimes sided with the engaged couple and refused to bless the marriage. Priests might also side with a couple that wished to marry against their parents' wishes. This was a way for the priests to remind parents that the church had more authority over family matters than the parents.

This family power structure changed in the New World. Colonial families were so far away from their mother country and so spread out, the church lost some of its authority over them. Additionally, colonists placed a higher value on women's contributions outside the home than Spanish society did back in the home country. Spain needed the labor of all its colonists, including women. Work outside the home gave colonial women more power within their families than Spanish women experienced in the Old World. Unlike women in Spain, Married women in the colonies enjoyed a more public life after their childbearing years ended.

The Chairman of the Board

Because strong families were critical to the success of every colony, controlling them was important. That supervisory, patriarchal role fell to the person at the head of the table: the father and husband.

The head of the family was second in importance to the colony's minister in the eastern colonies. If a father died, the eldest son or a male relative took his place. If no male relative was available, the widow supervised the family. However, widows of childbearing age were expected to remarry and start new families. Since all the colonies in the early days had fewer women than men, most young widows remarried quickly.

Urban families dealt with social problems—broken families, poverty, crime, drunkenness—until colonial governments later took over those roles. For example, if the death or absence of both a mother and father orphaned their children,

The most educated early American colonists were usually male ministers and lawyers.

church and town officials found families for them. They placed such children in the homes of "good" families with a strong head of household. This might have been the family of the children's relatives. If kinfolk were unavailable, the town's fathers or minister pressured the head of non-related families to take in orphans. That head of the family was expected to pass on his family's traditions and values to the adopted children. Often, the head of the household trained the adopted child in his own occupation or arranged for such training. The town's male leaders sometimes removed children from unsuitable families due to poor, alcoholic, absent, or criminal parents. The townsmen then found better families for the children. In these ways, family life was held up by the colonies as the model way to live.

Men had the last word on important family matters such as religion, work, and marriage. The married man's obligation was to provide everyone in his household with food and shelter. In exchange, he demanded that family members be hardworking, pious, and obedient. Wives and mothers were helpmeets, and were expected to enforce these values.

The "Helpmeete"

As the unequal assistant, or helpmeete, to "the head of the table," a wife's place in the colonial family was clear. When a woman married, any property she owned or money she had then belonged to her new husband. During the marriage ceremony, women vowed to support and obey their husbands. A married colonial woman had no legal rights separate from her husband. English colonists imported some parts of **common law**. William Blackstone wrote in 1765 in his *Commetaries on the Laws of England*:

> By marriage, the husband and wife are one person in law: that is, the very being or legal existence of the woman is suspended during the marriage, or at least is incorporated and consolidated into that of the husband; under whose wing, protection, and cover, she performs everything.

Colonial women shared with their husbands the power of supervising the education of their children, especially that of religion.

Colonies were always pressed for labor. As a result, colonial women were more often valued for their work contributions outside the home than women back in England and Europe. Colonial city women had the freedom to run businesses. Some served as their husbands' business associates. In fact, a widow was allowed to continue her deceased husband's business. Women could be shopkeepers, **midwives**, doctors, innkeepers, and tavern keepers. Educated widowed and married women could run **dame schools** to educate small children from their homes. In these urban occupations, women participated in public life far more than their more housebound countrywomen in the Old World.

However, frequent childbearing came first. Over a period of twenty years

Colonial marriages often joined property-owning families as well as the couple.

or so, bearing children and raising them kept women close to home. Even after their childbearing years ended, older mothers assisted in the care of their grandchildren and often, their own aging parents.

When children were old enough to marry, parents strongly supervised the matches. Male suitors who wanted to marry had to be financially independent. Otherwise the father of the girl's family would not allow the **courtship** to continue. Since the head of the family owned property that would be passed on at his death, or even beforehand, the father had a great deal of power over a young couple. Men and women did marry both with and without parents' approval. Soon they too started new families, which would populate cities far into the future.

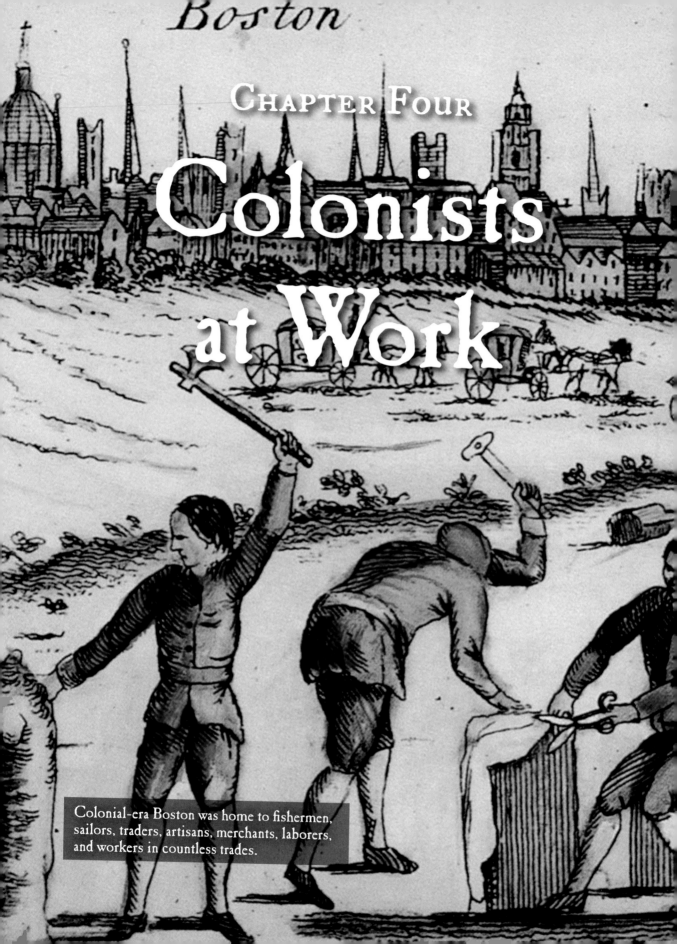

CHAPTER FOUR

Colonists at Work

Colonial-era Boston was home to fishermen, sailors, traders, artisans, merchants, laborers, and workers in countless trades.

"Every Christian ordinarily should have a calling. That is to say, there should be some special business, and some settled business, wherein a Christian should for the most part spend the most of his time; and this, that so he may glorify God by doing of good for others and getting of good for himself."
—Minister Cotton Mather, 1701

When it came to work, an American colony was no place for slackers. The success of all the colonies depended on everyone pitching in. Colonists had to feed themselves. Many learned to farm, fish, or hunt even if these were not their occupations "back home." The new continent was rich with natural resources, but the original colonists needed much more labor beyond their own to turn those resources into food, materials, and goods.

Colonies needed workers to turn flax into linen, weave clothes, forge iron and glass; and make bricks, pottery, and barrels. Skilled laborers were required to turn lumber into construction materials, houses, ships, tar, or pitch. Farming, fishing, hunting, building, hauling, cutting down trees, and mining required lots of brute labor. Whether colonists lived in the country or city, their daily lives required endless drudgery: feeding livestock, fetching water and wood, building and tending fires, cooking; cleaning dishes, pots, clothes, streets, and privy toilets.

Because labor needs became so great, town officials and the church frowned on anyone who did not work. In 1648, a Massachusetts General Assembly law read: "Householder or other shall spend his time idly or unprofitably under pain of such punishment as the Court of Assistants or County Court shall think meet to inflict." In many towns and cities, if a stranger showed up and did not find work, the town **constable** told him to leave town or face arrest or a fine. If parents were unemployed and poor, city or church officials found **apprenticeships** for their children as soon as they were old enough.

If someone lacked the will to work, colonial cities sent that person to a workhouse. One Boston workhouse in the mid-1700s housed between forty and fifty men and women at a time in separate quarters. A master and mistress lived on the ground floor as a family model for the workhouse inmates. They followed a strict schedule of work and prayers. Days started early and ended with an evening curfew. Inmates worked at jobs that needed to be done in the city, sometimes on a town farm. Artisans who needed help occasionally borrowed workhouse inmates, who lived at the workhouse for an average of about two years. Records are not clear on whether the workhouse system turned the unemployed into hardworking colonists. However, the workhouse got the message across: Everyone must work.

Large families and indentured servants could not keep up with the American colonies' need for labor. The message went out to the Old World: Send us more workers.

England, Europe, and West Africa got the message. They loosened **emigration** rules for skilled workers and laborers. Carpenters, shipbuilders, glassmakers, silversmiths, blacksmiths, weavers, barrel-making coopers, and other skilled workers crossed the Atlantic throughout the 1600s. They landed on city shores where they found higher wages than in their native countries. They discovered that training and reaching the upper levels of their crafts was an easier climb than at home. Owning land or starting businesses was easier as well. By the mid-1700s, so many skilled workers had left England for the Americas that the government slowed emigration of its most skilled artisans.

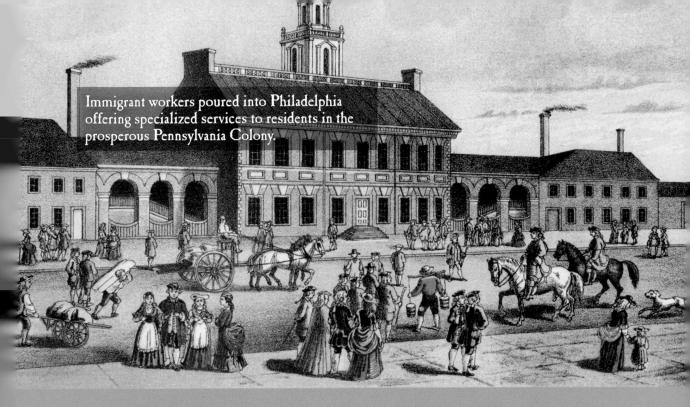

Immigrant workers poured into Philadelphia offering specialized services to residents in the prosperous Pennsylvania Colony.

THE BUTCHER, THE BAKER, THE BLOODLETTER?

Colonists' occupations included butchers, bakers, candlestick makers, blacksmiths, dressmakers, printers, and cobblers. Some of these jobs seem as strange now as a disc jockey or professional car racer would seem to a colonist. Can you guess what these colonial jobs were? Some of them still exist but under different names.

PONDERATOR	TIPPER
POYNTER	TONSER
RATONER	VAT MAKER
SHEPSTER	WET GLOVER
SPURRIER	WINDSTER
SLATER	

ponderator=a worker who checked weights and measures; poynter=a lacemaker; ratoner=a rat catcher; shepster=a female clothing pattern cutter; spurrier= a worker who crafted spurs for riding a horse; slater= a worker who put on roof slates; tipper=a worker who put on arrow tips; tonser=a barber; vat maker=a worker who dumped liquids into vats; wet glover=a leather glove maker; windster=a silk winder

Colonial city streets rang with the sounds of peddlers selling everything from knives to oysters.

However, England continued to rid its cities of criminals and debtors, along with the poor, unemployed, and homeless by sending them across the Atlantic. For the price of a ticket, many emigrants from Europe, England, and West Africa became part of the colonial indentured servant system. This bound these newcomers to colonial masters for years at a time.

However, indentured servants could not satisfy the need for thousands of laborers to work in mines or on plantations. So the colonies developed another labor system: slavery. No contracts, no pay, and no freedom were the circumstances for African slaves primarily on farms and plantations during the late 1600s until the end of the Civil War (1865). The much smaller percentage of colonial city slaves gained freedom from their bondage sooner since Northern Colonies depended less on the slave system.

MOVING UP

Except for slaves, emigrants who came from the Old World left countries with rigid class systems. Royal and church leaders had their place at the highest levels with the poor at the lowest. In between were military officers, landowners, lawyers, doctors, merchants, artisans, teachers, farmers, and laborers. In the Old World, most people remained in the same classes throughout their lifetimes.

These rigid social groups loosened in colonial cities where many different people kept arriving. Church leaders continued to have influence in all the colonies, but kings, queens, and lords far away no longer influenced the colonists' daily lives. In the Southern Colonies, experienced plantation owners from Barbados had arrived with the wealth to develop land, sponsor indentured servants, or buy slaves for their new plantations. This small group of founding families started at the top, where they remained. Elsewhere, success in the American colonies came from hard work, not from inheritances, royal titles, or connections.

CHAPTER FIVE

Children in the City

Life was precarious in the colonies for newborns, who were "as delicate as a bubble."

SEPTEMBER 6, 1709

"About one o'clock this morning my wife was happily delivered of a
son, thanks be to God Almighty. I was awake in a blink and rose and
my cousin Harrison met me on the stairs and told me it was a boy. We
drank some French wine and went to bed again and rose at 7 o'clock."

JUNE 3, 1710

"I rose at 6 o'clock and as soon as I came out news was brought that
the child was very ill. We went out and found him just ready to die
and he died about 8 o'clock in the morning. God gives and God takes
away; blessed be the name of God. ... My wife was much afflicted but
I submitted to His judgment better, not withstanding I was
very sensible of my loss, but God's will be done."
—WILLIAM BYRD II, FOUNDER OF RICHMOND, VIRGINIA

The birth and death of a child were never far apart in colonial times.
Both took place at home. One in five mothers died during childbirth. This put a newborn at risk of death too, because the infant,
without a mother, could not breastfeed. Diseases such as smallpox
and measles were deadly threats to everyone but especially to babies and children. Modern sanitation practices were hundreds of years away. Life-threaten-
ing germs killed many colonial-period mothers and their newborns within days
of birth. A young child was "as delicate as a bubble," poet Anne Bradstreet said
after her young granddaughter died.

The childbirth death rate was particularly high in the Chesapeake colonies
of Maryland, Virginia, and the Southern Colonies. Tropical illnesses weakened,
sickened, and killed Southern settlers in high numbers throughout the colonial
period. Since life spans were short, few older family members lived long enough
to help the next generation when new babies were born.

The survival rate of the colonists was higher in the North. Though the majority of Northern colonists still lived in the countryside, distances to one another and to relatives in the cities were closer. That meant city families had relatives nearby to help when a new baby arrived. In turn, new mothers could give their newborns more attention and care.

Bringing Up Colonial Children

Colonists in the city were never far from their meetinghouses, or the sermons their ministers delivered about childrearing. Bonding time between a mother and her newborn was valued because a new mother could pass on certain values immediately. Puritan minister John Robinson said, "Children, in their first days, have the greater benefit of good mothers, not only because they suck their milk, [but] . . . their manners also, by being continually with them, and receiving their first impressions from them."

The Northern Colonies, where most cities were located, depended on trained, disciplined adults who could take up urban occupations. A strict childhood upbringing was held up as the model that would produce such adults. Robinson had stronger words about rearing older children. He advised parents: "Surely there is in all children (though not alike)
a stubbornness and stoutness of mind arising from natural pride which must first be in the first place broken and beaten down so that the foundation of their education being laid in humility. . . ." In the later colonial period, this sternness softened. Historian Bruce C. Daniels has said of the Puritan childhood: "At the end of the seventeenth century, children in the first decade of life were the persons most controlled by society; at the end of the eighteenth century, they were the persons most indulged."

The constant arrival of newcomers changed views about bringing up children. The Quakers of Philadelphia were far less stern with their children than the Puritans in the New England colonies. In cities, parents and children probably became acquainted with new neighbors who had different models of successful children. Childrearing practices grew less fear-based, emphasizing duty and love instead. Bending rather than breaking a child's will was a new approach. Self-control, rather than outside control, became a valued childhood trait as time passed.

Children at Work

Everyone but babies worked the six days of the week they were not in church. City children might be asked to pick up items at the store or check whether the post rider had dropped off a letter at the local inn. A mother might send a child to deliver a message to a father who worked on the wharves. Small children could fetch kindling, weed a kitchen garden, or sweep dust from the front hall. The linen trade in all the Northern cities of Boston, Newport, New York, and Philadelphia was so important even children's hands were needed in this industry. In 1640, Massachusetts and Connecticut passed laws that ordered parents to teach both boys and girls the spinning of flax into linen. Protective laws against child labor were two hundred years away.

School Days

Learning to read and write was literally homework even if a child did not attend an actual school. Many more occupations in cities than in the countryside required people to read, write, and perform simple math. City children observed this everywhere. They saw traders reading shipping forms and storekeepers writing up bills for their parents. They might pass a cooper's workshop and witness him measuring wood staves to make barrels. Butchers carefully weighed cuts of meat then added up the bill for a child to bring home. Reading and writing was done both at work and at home. Publishing businesses sprang up in colonial cities as more people wanted to read not only the Bible, but also newspapers and pamphlets. City children saw print materials wherever they went. Announcements and advertisements were posted on fences and meetinghouse doors.

Upper middle-class city children might have had a father, grandfather, or uncle who was a lawyer or minister. These relatives were always reading. Children in the lower classes might have had a mother or sister who helped in a store and needed to read customers' shopping lists or write them a bill.

Educating urban children in reading and math skills was important for their potential future occupations. Most colonies began to draw up some regulations about providing schools. However, towns only loosely enforced school attendance. Families often needed their children to work at home or at an outside job.

The major colonial cities of Boston, Newport, New York, Philadelphia, and Charleston had dame schools. These usually took place in the homes of widows who had enough education themselves to pass on. Middle-class families—called "the middlings"—paid fees for their children to attend dame schools. Poor city children were more likely to get a hands-on education, doing menial chores around the city. This might be chasing down animals on the commons or carrying messages back and forth between businesses. In this way, these children became educated in the ways of city work that needed doing.

From a young age, colonial children learned the skills families needed to survive.

For the few teenagers who attended universities, advanced studies began at age fourteen. Reverand Thomas Sheperd sent his fourteen-year-old off to Harvard College in 1672 with this stern advice:

> Remember . . . that tho' you have spent your time in the vanity of Child-hood; sports and mirth, little minding better things, yet that now, when come to this ripeness of Admission to the College, now is the time com, wherein you are to be serious, and to learn sobriety, and wisdom in all your ways which concern God and man.

Some daughters, and many middle-class sons not bound for college, took up apprenticeships around the age of fourteen. Parents paid room and board for their children to live in the homes of someone who could teach them a trade. Boston educators offered night classes to male apprentices so they could also receive an education in reading, writing, and math.

Some girls served apprenticeships by working in shops. Extended family members took in nieces to show them how to run a household and develop proper manners that would honor the family. Since colonial artisans often sold their goods from their homes, many wives and daughters handled the business side of such occupations. Some girls who stayed home also served a kind of apprenticeship in weaving and sewing occupations. Here is a 1775 diary entry of Connecticut's Abigail Foote on her life as a dressmaker:

> Fixed gown for Prude. Just to clear my teeth, Mended Mother's Riding Hood—Fixed two gowns for Welch's girls—Carded tow [fibers]—spun linen—Worked on Cheese Basket—Pleated and ironed—Read Sermon of Dodridges—Spooled a piece—milked the cow—spun linen and did 50 knots—Spun thread—Set a red dye—Spun Harness twine—Scoured the Pewter.

Poor children continued to work as well. Urban families sometimes took them in to give them the advantage of an apprenticeship. In the booming cities, adults guided children within the home, the church, and the working world until they were children no more.

CHAPTER SIX
Pastimes

In a land of abundant forests, nearly everyone owned a jackknife to carve useful household objects.

Thus by his genius and his jack-knife driven

Ere long he'll solve you any problem given,

Make you a locomotive or a clock,

Cut a canal or build a floating dock

Make anything in short for sea or shore,

From a child's rattle to seventy-four

Make it, said I, ay, when he undertakes it,

He'll make the thing and make the thing that makes it.

—MINISTER JOHN PIERPONT

Pastimes required extra time. This was something the first colonists could not spare as they built up their cities during the 1600s. Hobbies, music, dancing, games, sports, and reading for pleasure would accompany the 1700s and the prosperity that it ushered in. Money could buy the time of servants and assistants to do the work colonists had done by themselves in the 1600s.

Still, colonists did not suddenly start dancing on Sundays instead of going to church in the 1700s. They were still religious, hardworking, and thrifty. It is not surprising that some of the first hobbies colonists took up were work related. Since the American colonies were rich in lumber and needed thousands of wooden objects, most boys learned to whittle with jackknives. This was preparation for future work in the "jackknife industries," which were important in colonial cities. Whether or not a boy became a woodworker, handling a knife from a young age gave him the skill to create woodcarvings and other related items.

Colonists still had little spare time for socializing, so they often combined work with get-togethers. Quilting parties in the cities were easy to arrange with neighboring women and girls living so close by. Quilting was part of the colonists' thrifty ways—using scraps to make something new and beautiful from something used. Quilts might be made of worn sheets, old military uniforms, and threadbare coats. In the years leading up to 1776, women and girls used their spinning skills as a way to boycott British textiles: they competed in all-day "spinning bees." They held some bees at the minister's house and spun wool into homespun cloth. The women then donated their material to the revolutionary cause against Britain.

CELEBRATIONS

Many traditions dating back to American colonial times continue to this day. Colonists brought the Thanksgiving harvest celebration from England as a day of prayers and gratitude for good fortune. The firing of colonial guns at Christmastime is commemorated with New Year's Eve fireworks today. Twelfth Night customs came to the English and Southern Colonies. It was a twelve-day period after Christmas when colonists gave presents to servants.

FROM MEETINGHOUSES TO COFFEEHOUSES

Colonial cities continued to draw English and European immigrants throughout the late 1600s and the 1700s. Sailors, traders, wealthy overseas merchants, artisans, servants, and laborers poured into the cities. They needed food, drink, and public places to conduct business or to relax. The small, plain meetinghouses would no longer do. To meet the needs of colonists and newcomers alike, taverns, inns, and coffeehouses sprang up in all the colonial cities. In 1691, eleven Boston taverns had licenses to serve alcohol. By 1710, there were eighty-one.

Taverns and coffeehouses were the first "public houses" or "pubs" as they were known in England. Drinking alcohol was fairly common during a time when water-borne illnesses sickened people. Taverns served as community and business meeting places and often as mail drops. Tavern keepers made local and

In the 1770s, Philadelphia's Penny Pot Tavern was a place where locals and travelers could hear the many languages of foreigners arriving in port.

international newspapers available. If a tavern had a few beds to rent to travelers, they were called "ordinaries."

To attract the upper classes and British military officers, colonial taverns and coffeehouses often had names that suggested English royal connections: The Rose and Crown, The Royal Exchange, Crown Coffee House, the Coffee House at Queen Street, Sign of the King's Arms, the King's House. These public gathering spaces offered a place where friends and newcomers could come together in the new land across the Atlantic.

VIVA LA FIESTA!

For twelve years, two thousand Spanish colonists lived in exile from the colonial city of Santa Fe, which they had founded. They had been in retreat since the 1680 Native American Pueblo Revolt. Local Native Americans had taken over the city to protest their loss of religious and personal freedom. After multiple bloody battles, they forced the Spaniards to leave Santa Fe. The colonists then left for their Mexican territories near present-day Texas. There they prayed to the Blessed Virgin for their return to Santa Fe. In 1692, colonists retook Santa Fe from the Native Americans without bloodshed. They promised them religious freedom and no punishment for the revolt.

To thank the Blessed Virgin for answering their prayers, the Spanish colonists created a religious festival in her honor: la Fiesta de Santa Fe. The fiesta has been celebrated for more than three hundred years. During the fiesta, celebrants carry a statue of the Blessed Virgin in a procession to St. Francis Cathedral on Santa Fe's main plaza. Worshipers recite prayers to the Blessed Virgin, whom they call "la Conquistadora."

Music and dancing follow on the plaza just as King Philip II envisioned in the 1500s when he told colonists to set aside plazas for future Spanish fiestas.

LEISURE TIME

By the 1700s, some hardworking colonists had grown rich from worldwide trade in the goods and crops they produced. Great wealth created a new upper class in all the colonial cities. Wealthy English and Dutch colonists in New York had the money and time to spend on horses they raced for sport. Horse-drawn coaches and sleds set out in groups for country outings. One privileged woman in 1704 wrote in her diary that during her sledding outing in Manhattan she "met with 50 or 60 sley." Ice skating was as popular a pastime for the Dutch colonists in New York as it had been in Holland.

Private clubs with membership fees came into existence in every colonial city. These clubs occasionally hosted traveling musicians and actors who performed for wealthy members. Mineral springs health spas were created to serve the leisured upper classes.

The middle classes enjoyed outings as well. Bowling greens for playing ninepins opened in the commons of Boston, Newport, and New York. Even those who did not own a stable of horses owned sporting guns and fishing reels. Hunting, fishing, and boating were popular in all the colonies since abundant forests and streams were not far from the cities.

Dinner parties, teas, and "frolicks" caused some church leaders to complain about frivolous gatherings. Minister Cotton Mather, in 1711, became distressed when he discovered that "a number of young people, of both Sexes, belonging, many of them, to my Flock, who have had on Christmas-night, this last Week, a Frolick, a reveling Feast, and Ball."

It was too late for the "old lions" in the meetinghouse to lecture the richer, freer colonists who had earned their leisure time in the 1600s. They began to spend it in the 1700s.

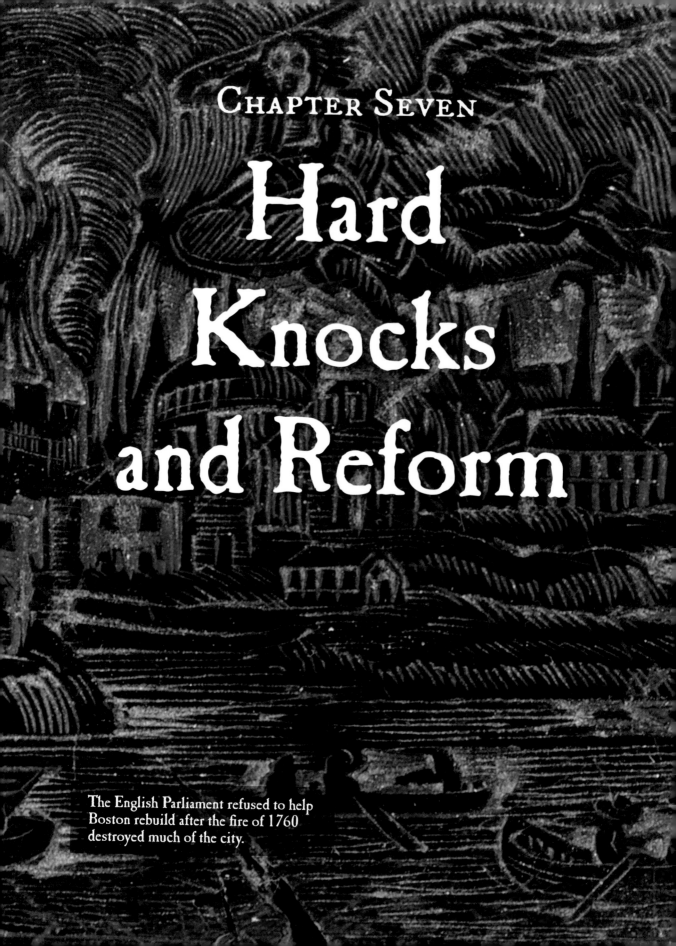

CHAPTER SEVEN

Hard Knocks and Reform

The English Parliament refused to help
Boston rebuild after the fire of 1760
destroyed much of the city.

"It seems to be now become dangerous to the good People of this City, to be out late at Nights, without being sufficiently strong or well armed, as several Attacks and Disturbances have been lately made in our Street."

—A New York Newspaper in 1749

The prosperous 1700s were not all years of frolic and ninepin bowling on the city commons. Expanding populations brought about growing pains. This is a view of what the public face of early colonial cities resembled at different times and places during the colonial period:

Residents fought for space and safety on dusty or muddy unpaved streets. They dodged unleashed dogs, garbage, human and animal waste, construction debris, horses, wagons, and livestock when crossing filthy streets. They had to shout to be heard over the yelling of dockworkers, cart drivers, and horseback riders coming through. Buildings that depended on fire for light and heat often caught fire, burning down entire neighborhoods. The economic success of the colonies left growing numbers of poor people behind. Waterborne diseases such as typhus and cholera sickened city populations in regular **epidemics**.

Yet Europeans and English immigrants continued to arrive. After all, their own big cities suffered these same conditions without the American colonial prosperity. Colonial cities underwent rapid growth and expansion after settlement in the 1600s, so much so that they had to scramble in the 1700s to regulate problems. Their success depended on it.

Getting Around

William Penn of Philadelphia, Sir John Ashley of Charles Town, and some Spanish colonists laid out the streets of their towns in a checkerboard grid pattern before anyone moved in. New Amsterdam arranged its city in the grid pattern as it expanded. Boston and Newport lagged behind the other eastern colonies with their streets. Instead private individuals dug out paths where and when they needed them. This haphazard approach to road building held back their economic success.

With expansion, urban colonial leaders realized they needed to plan additional roads and take care of them. The early roots of government and taxation soon followed. Colonists in all their cities argued about how to build, maintain, and pay for new roads. Their economic success depended on efficient travel. City leaders appointed officials and councils to handle transportation needs. Without such oversight, the major colonial cities of Boston, Newport, New York, Philadelphia, Charles Town, and Albuquerque might have remained settlements with a few cow paths and Native American trails running through them.

Regulating traffic was the next challenge. None of the colonial cities had police forces or traffic rules. Residents building houses and installing their own drains left rocks and debris in the roads. Riders and horse-drawn carriages barreled through streets without much regard for pedestrians. With few paths to transport building materials, laborers pushed through the streets with tottering wheelbarrows and carts. Fed up with the chaos, Bostonians levied fines on reckless horseback riders after "a very great hurt done to a childe, by reason of exceeding fast and hard riding of horses."

The building of wharves and docks soon followed as cities grew in the late 1600s. Running cargo in and out of anchored ships in small "lighters" was inefficient and costly. Private merchants in Boston and other cities built up their own waterfronts. These private facilities soon needed official regulation, as did the harbors. The colonies competed with each other to offer traders the best ports. Regulations about boat traffic, docking, and water safety contributed to a port city's success.

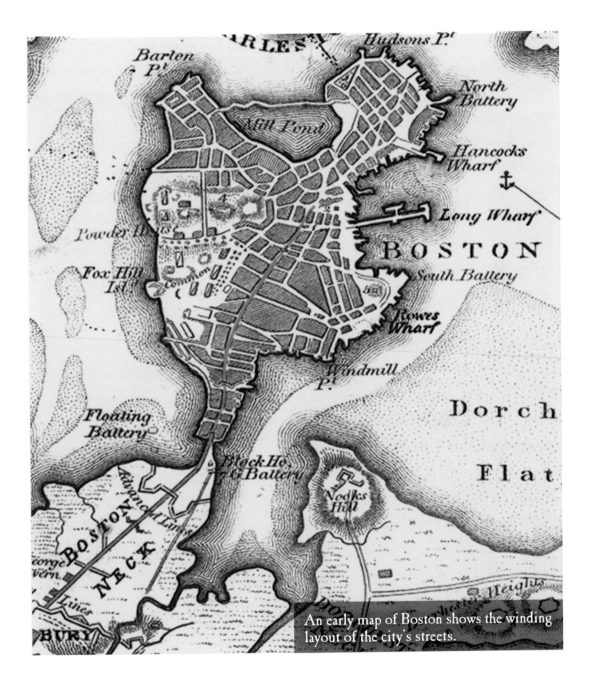

An early map of Boston shows the winding layout of the city's streets.

FIRE! FIRE!

Cities during the entire colonial period were firetraps. Many colonists were crowded in wooden houses. They stored gunpowder in homes, and built cooking and heating fires beneath sooty chimneys. The cities lacked official fire departments. Colonists were rightfully terrified of fire.

After several destructive fires, colonial cities developed fire prevention and firefighting measures. They discussed how to fight fires they could not prevent. Residents were required to have fire buckets and serve on firefighting teams in several colonial cities. Towns levied fines and punishments against those who did not clean their chimneys or who started fires as a result of careless acts.

Every colonial city developed requirements to use stone and brick for houses. Colonial cities began to tax their residents to purchase the latest in firefighting equipment. They built wells, pumps, and drains throughout their cities to fight the fires that did break out. Philadelphia, the best-organized and laid-out city, suffered the fewest fires. Boston, with its haphazard and narrow streets, suffered the most. Boston widened its streets after its mammoth fire of 1760, which nearly burned down the entire city.

CRIME AND PUNISHMENT

In the early colonial years, colonists had more to fear from outside attacks than from criminals. Strict, watchful families and church leaders kept a town's residents in line. Subjecting one to public shaming, especially if done before people the troublemaker knew, was another way to control behavior. Public whippings, being displayed in public "stocks," and being dunked in a "ducking stool" were all humiliating colonial punishments imported from England.

Public shaming had limitations as more strangers appeared in the colonies. Some criminals were runaways escaping violence or slavery from the countryside or other cities. Others were criminals England permanently sent to the colonies as punishment for crimes they had committed. British soldiers on leave from fighting colonial wars and defending the colonies caused trouble.

In the colonial port cities, most troublemakers were sailors. They came ashore looking for food, drink, games, and good times. Port cities adopted strict curfews for sailors who were supposed to return to their ships at night. Most cities had a small number of paid night watchmen. They walked through the cities looking for people violating curfews. They watched out for fires and broke up fights in streets, taverns, and homes. However, so few night watchmen were on patrol that they were ineffective in controlling crime.

City leaders realized that it was time to copy law enforcement methods from their original home countries. Spanish colonists used their military to control crime. In Dutch New Amsterdam, appointed **civilian** officers, called "schouts," were responsible for keeping order. English colonies initially forced civilian constables to do a job that few wanted. Despite the fines imposed should the position be rejected, ten out of seventeen constable appointees

d Newgate Prison, near Hartford, Conn.

The Connecticut Colony's Old Newgate Prison, built in 1705, imprisoned English soldiers and Loyalists as well as criminals as the American Revolution grew near.

2563

refused the job. The position entailed rounding up troublemakers, many of them sailors, and sending them home or back to their ships. Drunken friends and sailors were known to gang up on the constable, schout, or night watchman and rough him up. Again, the well-organized, practical Philadelphians created a system that worked. They taxed residents to pay constables and neighborhood watchmen to coordinate police work. Other colonial cities soon copied this successful crime-busting system. Paid security was the origin of our modern police forces.

As the colonies grew wealthier, they became attractive to burglars, robbers, and counterfeiters. Controlling criminals proved difficult. Colonists were reluctant to tax themselves for building prisons. The first broken-down jails served more as places of detention until a criminal came to trial. **Magistrates** often sent criminals to poor houses as a solution. This exposed poverty-stricken adults and children to criminals. By the mid-1700s, colonists finally taxed themselves enough to build secure prisons separate from the workhouse and **almshouse** systems.

Alms for the Poor

Old World methods for dealing with poverty travelled with colonists to the New World. Illness, disability, and loss of family support created conditions for poverty even in the prosperous colonies. At first, the small numbers of poor meant solutions were simple. Churches and the town offered the poor a small amount of public charity.

With waves of newcomers, numbers of poor colonial residents grew. Colonial cities needed to explore different solutions. First, they made sure that those unable to support themselves actually lived in the city. If not, they had to leave town. Public officials and church leaders applied pressure to make other family members responsible for taking in their poor relatives. If the poor person lived in the community without family help, the city might offer "out relief." The cities paid families with spare room to take in poor people. In this way, a solid family structure was upheld as a model for the poor. If children were old enough

American colonists modeled their urban poorhouses after English almshouses.

to work, officials and churches helped them find apprenticeships. This method modeled the value that hard work was the way out of poverty. By the late 1600s, all major cities in the English and Spanish American colonies had some form of a workhouse. Successful business leaders often supervised the workhouses to ensure that strong work habits were being modeled and enforced.

The almshouse was another institution for the poor. One Massachusetts colonist described a town's poorhouse as follows:

Good Old Almshouse

Shelter from the storm

Keeping warm its inmates old Infirm, ragged, poor;

Never closed was its door

Ever a comfort from the cold

Keeping every selectmen warm

Good Old Almshouse

The almshouse housed poor people who could not work and who were without families to take them in. This included the elderly, orphans, widows, and unmarried women with children, and the sick or disabled. Cities and churches collected funds to support almshouses.

Colonial solutions to poverty were imperfect, but in many ways they provided models for work and family values. The combination of out relief, workhouses, and almshouses kept many people off colonial streets.

Public Health

The New World colonies had new opportunities to build and create healthy communities from the start. However, at first they continued some of the same unhealthy practices people followed in the Old World. Knowledge about the importance of sanitation, however, was limited in both the old and new worlds.

In the early days of colonial cities, scavenging pigs allowed to roam city streets could not keep up with the amount of waste thrown out by residents and businesses. The roaming pigs caused traffic problems and left their own filthy wastes in the streets. Many towns paid a "hogreeve" to round up hogs, return them to their owners, and give them a fine. However, the practice of using pigs as a means of garbage removal continued. It was less expensive for owners to allow their pigs to feed on street garbage than to build pigpens and feed them at home.

Organic filth was everywhere. Butchers chucked animal innards out their doors. Some residents dumped crude toilets called "chamber pots" directly into streets and drains. Nonorganic rubbish and construction materials clogged the few streets of early colonial cities. Boston officials told residents to smooth out any dirt they dug up in the streets when they put in cellars and drains. Yet the city advised residents to dispose of their "beast entrails"—animal guts—by tossing them over the Mill Creek drawbridge.

Finally, the tidy Dutch in New Amsterdam had had enough. The filthiness of their public byways offended them. In 1657, they passed a regulation that forbade anyone from tossing "rubbish, filth, oyster shells, dead animal or anything like it" into waterways and streets. They developed laws about how humans and animals were to be buried: away from sources of drinking water where infectious germs could breed. Colonial cities vigorously enforced **quarantines**, which isolated sick people with infectious diseases from healthy residents. Ben Franklin promoted the idea of public hospitals to treat sick people and to keep them from infecting others. Only smallpox and yellow fever killed colonists in widespread epidemics. The colonies' public measures for controlling animal waste, building drains, draining swamps where mosquitoes bred, and controlling disease-bearing rats paid off. The health of American colonists put them far ahead of England and Europe by the mid-1700s.

REFORMS AND CHALLENGES AHEAD

As communications increased among the colonies, they shared new and improved solutions to public problems. Some historians argue that American colonial attitudes toward the poor were more charitable than those back in England and Spain. In less than a hundred years' time, the colonies had healthier people, lower crime rates, graceful buildings, smoother streets, and cleaner air than the English and European cities they had left behind.

Awareness of their successes made colonial leaders realize that they could solve the problems of their own colonies better than their home countries could. Communications among newcomers took place in countless newspapers, pamphlets, and public spaces. Strangers from different cities found it easier to share new and enlightened ideas about how to run their businesses and cities. By 1776, conversations about local matters shifted. Soon, colonial leaders decided that promoting a unified country of shining cities and productive agriculture was the next step. The American Revolution soon followed.

Glossary

almshouses

City houses where the homeless, poor, and sometimes criminals would stay.

Americas, the

Combined land masses of North and South America.

apprenticeships

Unpaid training periods for young people to learn a trade from skilled workers.

artisans

Skilled workers who make crafts by hand.

bastions

Four-sided watchtower forts taller than surrounding defensive walls.

Catholic

A member of a Christian religion which has its center in Rome.

civilian

A person not in the military or serving on a police force.

colony

A foreign settlement under the control of a distant country.

commerce

Business dealings and trade.

common law

A part of English law derived from custom.

commons

Land set aside in a village, town, or city for all residents to use.

constable

A security officer responsible for keeping the peace.

continent

A large, continuous land mass.

contract

A written or spoken legal agreement between two people or businesses.

courtship

The romantic relationship before marriage.

culture

Traditional ways of doing things; a society's values.

dame schools

Colonial schools for young children run in a woman's home.

emigration

The departure or export of people from one country to a foreign land.

epidemics

Outbreaks of infectious diseases that sicken large numbers of people at the same time.

grid pattern

An orderly design of city streets that intersect at right angles.

immigration

The arrival or import of foreign people to a new land.

indentured servants

Workers who are obligated by contract to work for someone for a certain period, usually in exchange for receiving travel and daily expenses.

magistrates

A town or city's law officers.

meetinghouse

A New England town building used as a church and public meeting place.

metropolis

A city.

midwives

Women experienced in delivering babies.

New World

All the islands and land masses in the western half of the world.

notary public

Legal representatives of a government.

Old World

African, Asian, and European lands in the eastern half of the world before Christopher Columbus reached the western half.

palisades

Wooden fences put up for defense.

patriarchal

Ruled by men.

plantation

A large estate that grows crops.

pueblo

A Native American village or city, mainly in the western Americas.

Puritan

A member of a strict Protestant Christian religion.

Quakers

Members of a Christian movement whose members share equal power in preaching to one another about their spiritual beliefs.

quarantines

The isolation of sick people from the healthy population.

sloop

A sailing boat with one mast for one or more sails.

sponsors

Supporters who financially back the cause or actions of others.

urban

Relating to cities.

Western Hemisphere

The half of Earth made up of North America, Central America, and South America, and their surrounding waters.

Further Reading

Capaccio, George. *Life in Colonial America: Countryside in Colonial America.* New York, NY: Cavendish Square Publishing, LLC, 2014.

Colligan, L.H. *Life in Colonial America: The Government in Colonial America.* New York, NY: Cavendish Square Publishing, LLC, 2014.

Demos, John. *A Little Commonwealth: Family life in Plymouth Colony.* 2nd ed. New York, NY: Oxford University Press, 1999.

Dow, George Francis. *Every Day Life in the Massachusetts Bay Colony.* New York, NY: Dover Publications, 1988.

Earle, Alice Morse. *Home Life in Colonial Days.* Readaclassic.com, reprinted 2010.

Ellis, Carol. *Life in Colonial America: The Military in Colonial America.* New York, NY: Cavendish Square Publishing, LLC, 2014.

Hart, Albert Bushnell. *Colonial Children.* New York, NY: Macmillan, 1925.

Hawke, David Freeman. *Everyday Life in Early America.* New York, NY: Harper & Row, 1988.

Morley, Jacqueline and David Salaryia. *You Wouldn't Want to be a Colonist: A Settlement You'd Rather Not Start.* New York, NY: Children's Press, 2004.

Rushforth, Brett and Paul Mapp. *Colonial North America and the Atlantic World: A History in Documents.* New York, NY: Pearson Education, 2008.

Stockham, Peter. *Early American Crafts and Trades.* New York, NY: Dover Publications, 1976.

Taylor, Alan. *The Settling of North America, vol. 1.* New York, NY: Penguin Books, 2002.

Websites

Becoming American: The British Atlantic Colonies, 1690–1763 Cities and Towns

nationalhumanitiescenter.org/pds/becomingamer/growth/text2/text2read.htm

This website provides information on many facets of colonial life, including capsules on the four largest cities in the colonies.

The Colonial Family in America

web.campbell.edu/faculty/vandergriffk/FamColonial.html

Explore the many facets of life for families at the founding of the United States.

American Beginnings, 1492–1690

nationalhumanitiescenter.org/pds/amerbegin/settlement/settlement.htm

Learn more about the start of the colonial period as well as a wealth of study questions.

Almshouse, Workhouse, Outside Relief: Responses to the Poor in Colonial America

www.wsc.mass.edu/mhj/pdfs/turner%20summer%202003%20combined.pdf

Read a series of essays describing the efforts to help the poor in the colonies.

Selected Bibliography

Anderson, Virginia DeJohn. *New England's Generation: The Great Migration and the Formation of Society*. Cambridge, UK: Cambridge University Press, 1992.

Bridenbaugh, Carl. *Cities in Revolt: Urban Life in America, 1743–1776*. New York, NY: Knopf, 1955.

Bridenbaugh, Carl. *Cities in the Wilderness: The First Century of Life in Urban America, 1625–1742*. New York, NY: Oxford University Press, 1971.

Daniels, Bruce C. *Puritans at Play: Leisure and Recreation in Early New England*. New York, NY: St. Martin's Press, 1995.

Demos, John. *A Little Commonwealth: Family life in Plymouth Colony. 2nd ed.* New York, NY: Oxford University Press, 1999.

Diamond, Jared. *Guns, Germs, and Steel: The Fates of Human Societies*. New York, NY: W.W. Norton, 1999.

Dow, George Francis. *Every Day Life in the Massachusetts Bay Colony*. New York, NY: Dover Publications, 1988.

Earle, Alice Morse. *Home Life in Colonial Days*. New York, NY: The Macmillan Company, 1926.

Fisher, Sydney George. *Men, Women, and Manners in Colonial Times, vol. 1,* Philadelphia, PA: J.B. Lippincott, 1898.

Hawes, John M. and N. Ray Hiner. *American Childhood: A Research Guide and Historical Handbook.* Westport, Connecticut: Greenwood Press, 1985.

Hawke, David Freeman. *Everyday Life in Early America.* New York, NY: Harper & Row, 1988.

Kalm, Peter, *Peter Kalm's Travels in North America, The English Version of 1770.* New York, NY: Dover Publications, 1966.

Krawczynski, Keith. *Daily Life in the Colonial City.* Santa Barbara, California: Greenwood Press, 2013.

Mann, Charles. 1491: *New Revelations of the Americas Before Columbus.* New York, NY: Knopf, 2005.

Rushforth, Brett and Paul Mapp. *Colonial North America and the Atlantic World: A History in Documents.* New York, NY: Pearson Education, 2008.

Ryken, Leland. *Worldly Saints: The Puritans as They Really Were.* Grand Rapids, Michigan: Zondervan Publishing, 1986.

Thompson, John. *The Journals of Captain John Smith: A Jamestown Biography.* Washington, DC: National Geographic Publishing, 2007.

Turner, Jennifer. "Almshouse, Workhouse, Outdoor Relief: Responses to the Poor in Southeastern Massachusetts, 1740–1800." Historical Journal of Massachusetts 31, no. 2 (Summer 2003).

Quotation Sources

Introduction: Before There Were States

p. 4, www.newnetherlandinstitute.org/history-and-heritage/more-histori-cal-fun/dutch-treats/early-impressions-of-new-netherland.

p. 5, www.swarthmore.edu/SocSci/bdorsey1/41docs/02-las.html.

Chapter 1: From Settlements to Cities

p. 13, www.digitalhistory.uh.edu/disp_textbook.cfm?smtID=3&psid=3869.

p.15, nationalhumanitiescenter.org/pds/amerbegin/permanence/text2/Vir-giniaCure.pdf

p. 16, Bridenbaugh, *Cities in Revolt: Urban Life in America*, 1743–1776, p. 57.

p. 20, "*Town Planning Review*, vol. 48, July 1977, pp. 247–268.

Chapter 2: Public and Private Spaces

p. 26, Hawke, *Everyday Life in Early America*, p. 52.

Chapter 3: Family Life in the City

p. 31, www.spurgeon.org/~phil/mather/dut-par.htm

p. 37, Blackstone, *Commentaries on the Laws of England.* Vol. 1 (1765), pp. 442–445.

Chapter 4: Colonists at Work

p. 41, Ryken, *Worldly Saints: The Puritans as They Really Were*, p. 27.

Chapter 5: Children in the City

p. 47, www.eyewitnesstohistory.com/colonialplantation.htm

p.48, Robinson, *American Childhood*, p. 25.

p. 48, web.campbell.edu/faculty/vandergriffk/FamColonial.html

p. 51, Demos, *A Little Commonwealth: Family life in Plymouth Colony*, p. 35.

p. 51, Fisher, *Men, Women, and Manners in Colonial Times*, Volume 1, p. 275.

Chapter 6: Pastimes

p. 53, Earle, *Home Life in Colonial Days*, p. 306.

p. 57, Bridenbaugh, *Cities in the Wilderness: The First Century of Life in Urban America, 1625–1742*. Kindle Edition.

Chapter 7: Hard Knocks and Reform

p. 59, Bridenbaugh, *Cities in Revolt: Urban Life in America*, 1743–1776, p. 113.

p. 65, Duxbury Vertical File, Poorhouse file, Duxbury Town Hall, Duxbury, Massachusetts.

Index

emigration, 42
epidemics, 59, 67

grid pattern, 20, 60

immigration, 32–33
indentured servants, 32, 34, 42, 45

Laws of the Indies, The, 11, 20, 21, 23

magistrates, 64
meetinghouse, 13–14, 25–26, 48–49, 54, 57
metropolis, 8
midwives, 38

New World, 4, **10**, 12–13, 20, 28, 34, **35**, 36, 64, 66
notary public, 13

Old World, 4, 7, 23–24, 28–29, 36, 38, 42, 45, 64, 66

palisades, 9, 19
patriarchal, 35–36
plantation, 13, 32–33, **33**, 45
pueblo, 5, 11, 21
    Native American Pueblo Revolt, 56
Puritan, 25, 48

Quakers, 15, 32, 48
quarantines, 67

sloop, 18
sponsors, 5, 45

urban, 9, 15, **15**, 32–34, **33**, 36, 38, 48, 50–51, 60, **65**

Western Hemisphere, 5
workhouse, 42, 64–66

Author Biography

L. H. Colligan regularly visited her town's colonial-era site and enjoyed travelling back to that period with her family. She has also time-travelled to Jamestown, Williamsburg, Charleston, Plymouth, Deerfield, Philadelphia, Albuquerque, and Santa Fe. When driving, she will pull off the road for any burial ground that is at least a few hundred years old. Now a New Englander, she lives within biking distance of two colonial-era town commons. She is, however, grateful for the modern convenience of her computer and Kindle, which have helped her research the many nonfiction books she has written in science, health, history, and literature, as well as this book.